DR. JAY POLMAR

I0473855

28 Minutes
to *Faster Reading*

www.speedread.org

My Appreciation to:

Maui and Windward Community Colleges, Maui/Oahu, Hawaii

Santa Fe Community College, Santa Fe, NM

The Institute of Human Dynamics, Santa Fe, NM

Southwest Learning Centers, Inc., Santa Fe, NM

Northern New Mexico Community College, Espanola, NM

Scottsdale Community College, Scottsdale, Arizona

El Paso Community College, El Paso, TX

Dona Ana Branch Community College, Las Cruces, NM

Univ. of New Mexico, Los Alamos & Valencia Branches

Univ. of Oregon, Eugene, Alternative Education Division for assisting in this SPEED READING research program.

My special thanks to E.L. Kretschmar, a high school vice-principal (now retired), for his input, additions and great editorial skills. My thanks to the entire Speedread.org. staff, and volunteer staff for their diligent preparation of this newly designed version in English.

Jay C. Polmar Ph.D.,

Copyright 2000, J.C. Polmar, Ph.D. Speedread America. - http://www.speedread.org
No part of this publication may be reproduced or transmitted in any form
by an means, electronic or mechanical, including photocopy, recording, or
information storage and retrieval methods now known, or to be invented,
without the written permission of SPEEDREAD AMERICA, Inc. except by
a reviewer who wishes to quote brief passages in connection with a review
written for inclusion in an educational publication or radio or TV broadcast.

DR. J.C. POLMAR
info@speedread.org

INSTRUCTIONS:

1. Read the book. Learn the exercises.

2. Practice exercises daily. Do them faster everyday.

3. Speed read the book, everyday, to keep practicing.

4. Practice for 30 days and enjoy speed reading!

Table of Contents

SpeedRead.org

Office of Dr. Jay Polmar, founder
www.speedread.org
info@speedread.org

Good Morning

Thanks for your support to www.speedread.org. We are an not-for-profit organization of specialized educational research in Accelerated Learning Techniques.

This unique program was developed from 1979 to 1993, and I taught it live in classes to thousands of students throughout the Western US and Hawaii. Now, due to my surgical accident the course, is only available on-line. In 1997 the program was modernized to one hour of self-taught, techniques implemented in a process-oriented program . This program has sold thousands of copies.

Our techniques are without equal. They make it easier so that all can double and triple their reading, with simply a few minutes of practice every day. The techniques of Speed Reading are applicable in all the languages.

A interesting story was told by a Nuclear Physicist, that took the program at the University of New Mexico, Adult Education div., at the Los Alamos Branch. He studied the technique the previous night, and was disillusioned that his improvement was only 158% after his first practices. Of course, he was reading a foreign language (English) newspaper. He had been born and educated in Israel learning Hebrew. Frustrated, he picked up his native newspaper from Tel Aviv, in the Hebrew language, his native tongue, and "his new speed of reading was that he flew through the paper" three to four times faster.

In order to speed read in a second language, like in ESL (English like a Second Language), you must be patient, practice in your native language first to develop the techniques. Use the audio program to mentally prepare yourself, and practice, practice and practice.

Good luck with your program. We are sure that you will be a speed reading success.

Sincerely,

Jay C. Polmar

founder, retired

www.speedread.org

Chapter 1

TEST YOUR READING RATE

Use A Digital Watch, Or Watch With A Second Hand, To Time Your Reading Speed

Start Now

Dr. Jay Polmar's 7-1/2 hour course BE DYNAMIC THROUGH SPEED READING is for people who read large amounts of material. Perhaps they get frustrated when they can't keep up with all the interesting material that is continually released.

The world's writers produce written material at a rate so phenomenal that, even the most avid of readers struggle to keep up with them. With your SPEED READ book, our beginner's program, you'll double or even triple the amount you now read.

Your brain and mind are capable of understanding from 10,000 to 50,000 units of information every minute. One unit being equal to one word. This information is based upon somewhat old statistics. Based on new speed reading technology, as well as strides in brain and mind development, you can probably achieve phenomenal reading gains.

To establish a beginning baseline this test is taking place. And no matter what your reading speed is, it is very different from your potential as a SPEED READER.

The average high school graduate, when tested, reads about 250 words per minute. The college student reads at about 300 words per minute. But, no matter what your beginning reading speed, don't worry, it is only the beginning baseline.

When Dr. Polmar spoke to other scientists who experimented with improving the function of the human brain and mind, the scientists usually implied that they believed the the brain/mind potential is limitless.

At SPEEDREAD.org. we believe that the brain/mind has one restriction. The restriction is that the brain functions, as a result of, electrical-impulse energy mixed with oxygen through blood flow. The brain operates at all times as a sensing device (awareness) for your physical body. Therein lies the restriction, unlimited by brain and mind, we are physically limited by our human body. I guess we all can agree that our individual bodies have limitations.

All of us have heard, at sometime during our upbringings, that we are limited and probably won't achieve much in life. We are also aware that we, individually, have limits. You, I, and everyone, has also heard messages from home, school, and elsewhere that amounts to "You're dumb, stupid, an idiot; you'll never amount to anything".

Guess what? Those words have powerful effects, and do hold us back from success. Perhaps we'd all be wiser to forgive those who are foolish with the use of their words.

These are only what we hear in school and home. What about the messages from others? A jealous friend, a "hellfire and brimstone" church minister, or an army drill sergeant can all do damage to our personal self-esteem and our educational potential. But do not fear, these will not permanently damage your success potential unless you let them get to you.

Remember your body is a vehicle of sensing (five senses) for the brain and mind to survive, potentially even succeed. Our belief is that your brain and mind together work like a computer. The brain, is the hardware, and the conscious mind (the thoughts you consciously think) is the software. Perhaps the brain and mind are somehow connected to our physical body to make life convenient for us to learn certain lessons.

Obviously we learn through information (or data) which is communicated in many ways.

We get information through our five physical senses, and we make decisions. We make choices and judgments as well from the factors that our physical senses bring into play. We learn, not only from physical senses, but through various forms of thought. Most thought is conscious in nature. The five physical senses (sight, smell, hearing, taste, touch) are preprogrammed for automatic reaction.

An example of automatic reaction might be: when a hungry teenager smells pizza, he or she begins salivating. What's taking place is that the physical sense of smell (called olfactory senses) has automatically delivered a thought, PIZZA, to the brain and mind. The thought may be unconscious. Let me give you an example. Let's say you are upstairs studying in your bedroom when the doorbell rings and someone answers it.

You continue studying. Slowly the aroma of PIZZA creeps up the stairs and without thought you aim downstairs just as the last slice is being devoured by your younger brother. That's an unconscious reaction. If it were a conscious reaction, your younger brother might only get half the pizza instead.

One other thing to remember: Sensing food is a physical sensation through smell. It is a mental sensation (unconsciously or consciously) through thought.

And lastly it is a physical sensation through eating, swallowing, and smiling. To summarize the PIZZA adventure: Brain and mind is where the "action" is. Body is where the "reaction" is.

Back to reading: Our limitation, regarding reading speed, was first taught to us during our early childhood education. Then finally, we learned words and their sounds.

Usually this occurred during the first two or three years of schooling in the public school system. During those years we first became acquainted with letters, and their sounds. Then, later on we learned syllables and their sounds. Then finally, we learned words and their sounds.

You older students of life will remember: Dick and Jane played with Spot the dog.

Then, they taught us to read paragraphs aloud, carefully moving our lips, pronouncing each syllable and each word slowly. We were further taught to read sentences 'out loud'.

We carefully mouthed each syllable and each word slowly to the teacher and the class, and she said "Very good, you got it right".

After a few short years, classroom reading instructions effectively stopped. Yet, we were still mouthing each syllable and each word as we read; both aloud to others and silently to ourselves.

Because of the learning experience of reading syllables, out loud, then silently to ourselves we developed our average 250 word per minute reading limitation.

Yet researchers have consistently shown that a high school graduate, using the SPEED READ methods, usually doubles his or her reading speed and then goes on to improve even further.

Thousands have taken Dr. Polmar's seven-hour college speed reading course that this condensed version is based on.

We're very proud that the statistics have shown a 311% national improvement in reading rate from consistent use of these methods.

Scientists believe that there is no limit to the brain and mind capacity. No limits exist to how many thousand words per minute you can read. In fact, in the back section of this book you'll find two self-talk methods that'll help you increase reading speed, memory, comprehension, recall, and improve concentration.

There is one challenge that many people face while learning SPEED READING. It's that inner voice, that we all have, that actually races on while you are reading, or studying.

The field of anthropo maximology (maximizing human potential) calls that inner voice "The Babbler".

What it really is - is an internal, all too often negative, voice that is always busily at work.

It disrupts you when you are trying to read. It worries you before exams. And sometimes it babbles on and on and on, and that's a warning that you need help with shutting off the Babbler's voice. The Babbler is not your best friend although it sticks to you like superglue.

When you learn to shut-off the Babbler's voice, the speed at which you can speed read material into your brain and mind will be phenomenal.

Since the speed of brain/mind processing is probably unlimited, you'll be able to input reading data into your mind at accelerated rates using SPEED READING.

Students in speed reading classes have been tested at up to 8,000 words per minute. However, it takes much practice and diligence to reach those speeds.

An important fact to remember is that you will be unlearning bad reading habits and relearning the reading process. If you have had any trauma at school or at home regarding reading, (or even emotion related problems such as physical, emotional, mental or sexual abuse, etc.) it is very possible that an educational block may have also been programmed.

It is not our intent to suggest that SPEED READING is able to remove educational blocks caused by emotional trauma. If you need psychiatric or psychological help please get it.

SPEED READ can only help you override incorrect reading training from your early education and then retrain you.

To summarize: Your brain and mind have the ability to absorb thousands of bits of information per minute. And since you are probably reading much slower due to early education of individually mouthing syllables and words, you have this vast potential for speed reading development.

If you have been taught incorrect reading habits during childhood, know that from this moment on, you can retrain yourself as a powerful SPEED READING student striving for limitless success. And if you are confident in yourself, you can achieve anything.

STOP

READING

HERE!

COMPUTE YOUR READING SPEED

TOTAL NUMBER OF WORDS: 1,459

READING TIME: _____

Do the math. Divide number of words by reading time. You'll get the average words per minute _____

Two quick ways to see if you've got a motor-reading habit limiting you:

1. Pick up a newspaper or magazine and start to read silently. Put your open palm of one hand over your throat (Adam's Apple) while you read. If you feel contractions, you need to remedy this motor-reading function. See page 18-20 for the cure.

2. Take a newspaper or magazine to read silently to yourself. Do the same thing and put your open palm over your lips. If you feel movement, see page 18-20 for the cure.

Now the good news:

Two major benefits from
SPEED READING:

1. SPEED READING, due to the brain/mind and accelerated reading methods used in this course, means that what you read will be stored in long-term memory for later recall. We think this is amplified by intensified focus used in SPEED READING. Focus causes the states of consciousness to be altered, thereby accessing long-term memory.

2. The other facet is that eidetic (or photographic) memory, or auditory (tape recorder) memory often occurs. Humans have the potential to remember everything they've ever seen, read, or heard, even if they weren't paying full attention. Your brain and mind, which is like a computer, stores all memories.

"A great and beautiful invention is
memory, always useful both for
learning and for life..."
...from the Dialexeis, c. 400 B.C.

*I feel assured
there is
no such thing as
ultimate forgetting;
traces once impressed
upon the memory
are indestructible."*

... Thomas DeQuincy

NOTES

Chapter 2

"It is impossible for a man to learn what he thinks he already knows.

... Epitectus (50-138AD)

If you can read this, you can read it faster. And that's the bottom line!

You may have some doubts about this. You may think that this isn't possible; that you can only read so fast and that's the limit. THIS IS NOT TRUE. It is now possible for every person who can read, and who practices the methods in this book to double, even triple, his or her reading speed and improve comprehension.

IF YOU ARE A SLOW READER IT IS BECAUSE YOU READ WORD BY WORD, AND YOU SAY EVERY WORD TO YOURSELF.

INSTEAD, WHAT YOU NEED TO DO IS, USE YOUR HAND AS A PACING MACHINE AND GO THROUGH EACH PARAGRAPH SO FAST YOU DO NOT HAVE TIME TO STOP AT EACH WORD AND SAY IT TO YOURSELF.

WHAT YOU SEE, INSTEAD, ARE GROUPS OF WORDS THAT CARRY THE MEANING (WORDS BY THEMSELVES DO NOT) SO YOU WILL UNDERSTAND MORE OF ANYTHING THAT YOU READ.

The LEARNING DYNAMICS methods used in SPEED READ are intentionally redundant and repetitious! It is repetition, visualization, and various other techniques that you will be learning that will help you achieve the results you desire and be the best you can possibly be.

"You can teach a student a lesson for a day; but, if you can teach him to learn by creating curiosity; he will continue a day; the learning process for as long as he lives".
....Clay Bedford

What Kind of Reading Problems Do You Have?

Most people go back over words, phrases, and paragraphs because they think they've 'spaced out' or didn't understand what they read. This is called regressing.

READING REGRESSIONS are very common among readers. There are two types of reading regression. A 'conscious' regression is when you may feel that you didn't really understand something you read, so you "consciously" decide to go back and read it again.

'Unconscious' regressions, on the other hand, exist mostly because poor reading habits were formed when you first learned to read.

Unconscious regressions happen when your eyes unconsciously go back and look again at certain words or phrases. You'll end this habit using 28 MINUTES TO FASTER READING. First, answer these questions:

Question 1: Do you often go back and reread because you were daydreaming while your eyes continued to follow the lines automatically?

[ ] Yes [ ] No

Question 2: Do you often go back and reread because you lost the thought pattern of what you were reading, or you didn't understand what you read?

[ ] Yes [ ] No

Question 3: Do you often go back and reread because you've, somehow, lost your place and are trying to locate it again?

[ ] Yes [ ] No

If you answered 'yes' to any of these questions, a simple solution for you is: *DO NOT GO BACK AND RE-READ THE MATERIAL YOU'VE ALREADY READ!*

The material you think you've missed will either return to memory automatically, come back to you from contextual reading, or you may scan or review the paragraph or page again later. Just fold down the corner of the page, highlight the area, and go back to it after you've finished the chapter.

Our next reading problem is **SUBVOCALIZING.** Subvocalizing is mentally repeating what you've read in your own mind. Remember the test where we asked you to put the palm of your hand over your throat and over your lips while you read?

This is the test for subvocalizing. It simply demonstrates that either your throat muscles are contracting (as if you are speaking) or your lips are slightly moving.

The solution for subvocalizing is CHEW GUM or SUCK LIFESAVERS. This will keep subvocalization to a minimum and permit you to break the habit after a few days.

Another reading slowdown comes from **EYE FIXATIONS.** That's when you mentally stop, and your eyes fixate on a single word. That means you're stuck in one place.

The solution is to first read in groups of a few words, that have meaning. Then go for half-lines as your peripheral vision expands, then to whole lines, etc.

LESS READING FIXATIONS MEANS FASTER READING!

The next to the last challenge is called LACK OF RHYTHM. When practicing the reading coordination exercises found on pages 30-35 to develop eye-to-hand coordinated movement you'll accelerate your reading.

And finally, **THE POSITION YOU READ IN.** Most people are unaware how important it is for them to be sitting straight up in a chair when they read.

Might I suggest that you prop your book up at a 45o angle. If you sit at a table with the book at this angle you don't have to readjust it. Therefore you'll do much less work.

I've personally been asked by many students, "Can I read in bed and still comprehend and remember what I read?" My answer is, of course, you can read in bed if you don't mind losing efficiency, concentration, and memory. Research indicates if you study sitting up, you'll get better grades than studying in bed.

SPEED READING in bed isn't easy... Studying important information that way just isn´t smart

NOTES

Chapter 3

THE TECHNIQUE

You already own the greatest reading acceleration device that has ever been developed. It is simply your hand. People have spent thousands of dollars attempting to increase their reading speed. But no inventions or machines can do what your hand and your pacing finger can do for you to improve your reading speed.

What do your eyes do while you are "trying" to read? If you're like most people they are jerking around, looking around, bouncing here and there.

Then they will fixate for a moment or two and maybe move on again causing your brain to wonder what you're doing. Sound familiar? Untrained readers go through this often. We call this "trying" to read.

By learning the speedpacing movement you'll learn to control and accelerate your hand-to-eye coordination. This is called PACING.

This technique is vital for learning the method called SPEED READING.

Now place your index finger at the beginning of the following paragraph (under the first word). Then race it, your finger and eye together, to the end of the line.

Then go to the next line. Be sure you are comfortable with how you are doing this. You must work to develop eye and finger coordination

IF YOU ARE A SLOW READER IT IS BECAUSE YOU READ WORD BY WORD AND YOU SAY EVERY WORD TO YOURSELF.

INSTEAD WHAT YOU SHOULD DO, IS USE YOUR INDEX FINGER AS A PACER AND GO THROUGH THIS PARAGRAPH SO FAST YOU DON'T HAVE THE TIME TO STOP AT EACH WORD AND SAY IT TO YOURSELF.

WHAT YOU SEE INSTEAD ARE GROUPS OF WORDS THAT CARRY THE MEANING (WORDS BY THEMSELVES DO NOT).

SO YOU WILL UNDERSTAND MORE OF ANYTHING AND EVERYTHING YOU READ.

You read it faster. How did I know? Simple, everyone reads it faster! And you understood it more. These are only a few gains you will make with this program. Let's look at more. Look at this same paragraph below:

IF **YOU** ARE A **SLOW READER** IT IS **BECAUSE** YOU **READ WORD BY WORD** AND YOU SAY EVERY **WORD TO** YOURSELF. INSTEAD WHAT YOU SHOULD DO, IS **USE** YOUR **INDEX FINGER AS** A **PACER** AND **GO THROUGH** THIS **PARAGRAPH SO FAST YOU DON'T** HAVE THE TIME TO **STOP. AT EACH WORD** AND SAY IT TO YOURSELF.

WHAT YOU **SEE** INSTEAD ARE **GROUPS OF WORDS** THAT **CARRY** THE **MEANING** SO **YOU** WILL **UNDERSTAND MORE** OF ANYTHING AND EVERYTHING YOU READ.

See what I mean? The grayed out type is unnecessary for you to store in memory: You're retaining only important words ... the bold ones. So this is the message you get:

You ... slow reader ... because ... read ... word by word... say every word to self. Use ... index finger as pacing device ... go through ...paragraph... fast. Do not stop ... at word(s).

You see ... groups of words ...carry meaning. You ... understand more.

Sure it sounds like Tonto from the Lone Ranger series, but, you still got the message loud and clear.

As a DYNAMIC SPEED READER you will read, in just a fraction of the time that it took you before.

You'll develop excellent comprehension. You'll easily be able to use what you get from your reading. You'll understand the information and increase your memory and recall capacity in the process. You will study more effectively and get higher grades in school. You'll be better informed which will make you a better student, employee, communicator, and decision maker.

You'll cut reading time on reports, memos, correspondence, newspapers, novels, nonfiction, magazines, etc. You'll save time, and time is money.

Another important factor in reading speed is:

READING CONDITIONS. - Determine exactly what you need to read properly. A hi-liter? If you are using a computer, do you have the machine turned on to the right program, games turned off and, are you ready to proceed?

You'll need a cool drink during warm weather (water, fruit juice). You'd also better visit the bathroom before you start reading. Remove or unplug:

- Magazines, unless being used as a part of what you are going to read.
- TV (except for educational programs). Stereo, radio will cause varied distractions. Turn them off.
- Brothers, sisters, friends, etc. are in the way when you are reading.

- Mate, spouse, lover. They easily can dissuade you from reading.
- Food can break your concentration and reading patterns.
- Alcohol - don't even go there. Drinking and studying is a sure fire failure.
- Cigarettes will fog your thinking abilities...nicotine is a drug.
- Marijuana - don't go there either. A foggy brain is useless in an exam.
- Take the phone off the hook. Put out the dog or cat.
- Create a quiet reading/study space. You might want music playing; use soft, classical, meditation' oriental or other forms of relaxing music. Play it very softly.
- This sounds pretty extreme, however, modify it for pleasure reading, early morning newspapers, or corporate magazines.

SPEEDPACING

USING YOUR PACING FINGER.

To use your pacing finger to increase your reading speed simply extend your index finger; then run the tip of that index finger along each line of type, just underneath the words you are reading.

As you move your finger, read just above it and coordinate your eyes with your pacing finger.

When your finger comes to the end of the line, lift it up about half an inch and move it rapidly to the beginning of the next line and repeat the process. This may seem awkward at first, yet the awkwardness will quickly pass. And almost as soon as you begin using your finger for pacing, your reading speed will dramatically increase.

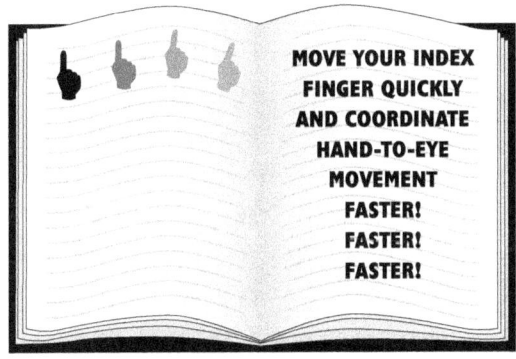

This pacing technique actually helps eliminate unconscious regression. That alone can actually double your reading speed. It will take you some practice and time to achieve this acceleration; but it's worth it.

Practice first with coordinating your eyes and index finger with the pages of X's that follow. After you practice this exercise we'll get into some more serious techniques.

Practice this exercise for five minutes each day. Build more coordination between your eyes and your index finger (pacer).

This improves your reading speed. In addition, when your are reading 2,000 words per minute your eyes will not need the finger index as pacer. By then your eyes and your mind will be very well trained.

Xxxxxxx xxx xxxxxx xxxxxxxx xxxxxx xxxxx xx xxx xxxxxx x xxxxx xxxx xx. Xxxxxx x xxxxx x xxxxx. Xxxxxx

   a.   xxx x xxxxx xxxxx x xxxxx x xxxxxx x xxxxx. Xxxxxx x

   b.   xxx xx x xxxx. Xxxxx xxx xx xxx x xxxx xx xx xxxxx xxxxx

   c.   xxx xx xxx xxx xx xx xxxxx xxxx. Xxx xxxx xx xxx xxxx x xxxxx xxxxx xx xxx xxxx xx xxxxx xxxx.

Xxx x xxxxx. Xxxxxx x xxxxx x xxxxx. Xxxxx xxxxx xxx x xxxx xxxx xxxxx xxxxx xxxxx x xxxxx. Xxxxx xxxxx xx? Xxxxx x xxxxx x xxxxx!

Xxx xxxxx xxxxx xxx x xxxx xxxx xxxxx xxxxx xxxxx x xxxxx xxxxx xxxxx xx xxxx. Xxx xxxx xx xxxxxxx x xxxxxxxxxx xx xxx xxxx xx xxxxx xxxx. Xxxx x xxxxx. xxxxx x xxxxx x xxxxx. Xxxxx xxxxx xxx x xxxx xxxx xxxxx xxxxx xxxxx x xxxx xxxxx xxxxx xxxxxx.

Xxxxxxx xxx xxxxxx xxxxxxxx xxxxxx xxxxx xx xxx xxx x xxxxx xxxxxx x xxxxx x xxxxxx x xxxxx. Xxxxxx x xxx xx x xxxx. Xxxxx xxx xx xxx x xxxx xx xx xxxxx xxxxx xxx xx xxx xxx xx xx xxxxx xxxx. Xxx xxxx xx xxx xxxx x xxxxx xxxxx xx xxx xxxx xx xxxxx xxxx. Xxx x xxxxx. Xxxxxx x xxxxx x xxxxx. Xxxxx xxxxx xxx x xxxx xxxx xxxxx xxxxx xxxxx x xxxxx. Xxxxx xxxxx xx? Xxxxx x xxxxx x xxxxx!

Xxx xxxxx xxxxx xxx x xxxx xxxx xxxxx xxxxx xxxxx x xxxxx xxxxx xxxxx xx xxxx. Xxx xxxx xx xxxxxxx x xxx xxx read xxxxx xx xxx xxxx xx xxxxx xxxx. Xxxx x xxxxx. xxxxx x xxxxx x xxxxx x xxxxx faster. Xxxxx xxxxx xxx x xxxx xxxx xxxxx xxxxx xxxxx x xxxx xxxxx xxxxx xxxxxx.

Xxxxxxx xxx xxxxxx xxxxxxxx xxxxxx xxxxx xx xxx xxxxxx x xxxxx xxxx xx. Xxxxxx x xxxxx x xxxxx. Xxxxxx xxx x xxxxx xxxxxx x xxxxx x xxxxxx x xxxxx. Xxxxxx x xxx xx x xxxx. Xxxx xxx xx xxx x xxxx xx xx xxxxx xxxxx xxx xx xxx xxx xx xx xxxxx xxxx. Xxx xxxx xx xxx xxxx x xxxxxxxxx xx xxx xxxx xx xxxxx xxxx. Xxx x xxxxx. Xxxxxx x xxxxx x xxxxx. I can xxxxx xxx x xxxx xxxx xxxxx xxxxx xxxxx x read faster xxxxx. Xxxxx xxxxx xx? Xxxxx x xxxxx x xxxxx! Xxx xxxxx xxxxx xxx x xxxx xxxx xxxxx xxxxx xxxxx x xxxxx xxxxx xxxxx xx xxxx. I now can xxxx xx xxxxxxx xxxxxx xxxxx xx xxx xxxx xx xxxxx xxxx read faster. Xxxx xxxxxx. xxxxxx x xxxxx x xxxxx. Xxxxx xxxxx xxx x xxxx xxxx xxxxx xxxxx xxxxx x xxxx xxxxx xxxxx xxxxx. Xxxxxx xxx xxxxxx xxxxxxxx xxxxxx xxxxx xxxxx xx xxx xxxxx x xxxxx xxx xx. Xxxxxx x xxxxx x xxxxx. Xxxxxx xxx xx xxxxx. Xxxxx xxx xx xxx x xxxx xx xx xxxxx xxxxx xxx xx xxx xxx xx xx xxxxx xxxx. Xxx xxxx xx xxx xxxx x xxxxx xxxxx xx xxx xxxx xx xxxxx xx. Read faster. Xxx x xxxxx. Xxxxxx x xxxxx x xxxxx. Xxxxx xxxxx xxx x xxxx xxxx. Xxxxx xxxxx I do it xxxxx x xxxxx. Xxxxx xxxxx xx? Xxxxx x xxxxx x xxxxx!

Xxx xxxxx xxxxx xxx x xxxx xxxx xxxxx xxxxx xxxxx x xxxxx xxxxx xxxxx xx xxxx. xx xxxx Now I am xx xxxxxxx x xxxxx xxxxx xx xxx xxxx xx. Xxxx x xxxxx. xxxxxx x xxxxx x xxxxx.

Speed Reading xxxxx xxx x xxxx xxxx xxxxx xxxxx xxxxx x xxxx xxxxx xxxx. Xxxxxx xxx I read xxxx x xxxxx xxxx xx xxxxx x fast now xxxxx x xxxxx. Xxxxxx xxx xxxxx xxxxxx x xxxxx x xxxxxx x xxxxx. Xxxxx x xxx xx xxxxx. Xxxx xxx An avid SPEED READER xx xxx xxx xx xxxxxxx xxxx. Xxx xxxx xx xxx xxxx x xxxxx xxxxx xx xxx.

Xxx x xxxxx. Xxxxx x xxxxx I read x xxxxx xxxx fast. Everyday xxx x xxxx xxxx xxxxx xxxxx xxxxx x xxxxx. Xxxxx xxxxx xx? I am a faster reader!

Xxx xxxxx xxxxx xxx x xxxx xxxx xxxxx xxxxx xxxxx x xxxxx xxxxx xxxxx xx xxxx. I read fast. Xxxx xx xxxxxxx x xxxxx xxxxx xx xxx xxxx xx xxxxx xxxx. Everyday. Xxxxx faster and faster xxxxx xxx x xxxx xxxx xxxxx I am x xxxx xxx an avid reader. Xxxxxxx xxx xxxxxx.

Xxxx an avid reader. xxxxxxxx xxxxxx xxx SPEED READING is xxxxxx x xxxxx xxxx xx. Xxxxxx x xxxxx x xxxxx. Xxxxxx xxx xxxxxx easy to learn xxxxxx x xxxxx x xxxxxx x xxxxx. Xxxxxx x xxx xx x xxxx. Xxxx xxx xx xxx x xxxx xx xx xxxxx xxxxx. Xxxx xx xxx xxx xx! Xxx x xxxxx. Xxxxxx x xxxxx x xxxxx. Xxxx xxxxx xx? Xxxxx x xxxxx x xxxxx!

Xxx xxxxx xxxxx xxx x xxxx xxxx xxxxx xxxxx xxxxx x xxxxx xxxxx xxxxx xx xxxx. Xxx xxxx xx xxxxxxx x xxxxx xxxxx xx xxx xxxx xx xxxxx xxxx. Xxxx x xxxxx. xxxxxx x xxxxx x xxxxx. Xxxxx xxxxx xxx x xxxx xxxx xxxxx xxxxx xxxxx x xxxx xxxxx xxxxx xxxxxx.

Xxxxxxx xxx xxxxxx xxxxxxxx xxxxxx xxxxx xx xxx xxxxxx x xxxxx xxxx xx. Xxxxxx x xxxxxxxxxx x xxxxxxxx. Xxxxxx xxx x xxxxx xxxxxx x xxxxx x xxxxxx x xxxxx. Xxxxxx x xxx xx x xxxx. X xxx xxx xx xxx x xxxx xx xx xxxxx xxxxx xxx xxx xx xxxx. Xxx xxx xxxx xx xxxxx xxxx.

Xxx x xxxxx. Xxxxxx x xxxxx x xxxxx. Xxxxx xxxxx xxx x xxxxxx. Xxxxxx xxxxx xxxxx xxxx. Xxxxx xxxxx xx? Xxxxx x xxxxx x xxxxx?

Xxx xxxxx xxxxx xxx x xxxx xxxx xxxxx xxxxx xxxxx x xxxxx xxxxx xx x xxxxx xxxxx xx xxx xxxx xx xxxxx xxxx.

Xxxx x xxxxx. xxxxxx x xxxxx x xxxxx. Xxxxx xxxxx xxx xxxxxx xxxxx xxxxxx. Xxxxxxx xxx xxxxxx xxxxxxxx xxxxxx xxxxx xx xxx xxxxxx x xxxxx xxxx xx. Xxxxxx x xxxxx x xxxxx. Xxxxxx xxx x xxxxx xxxxxx x xxxxx x xxxxxx x xxxxx. Xxxxxx x xxx xx x xxxx. Xxxx xxx xx xxx x xxxx xx. Xxx xxxxx xxxxx xxx xx xxx xxx xx xx xxxxx Xxx Xxxxx xx xxx xxxx x xxxxx xxxxxxxxxxx xxxxxxxx xxxxxxx xx xxx. Xxxxxx x xxxxx x xxxxx. Xxxxxxxxxx xx xxxxxxxxxxx. Xxxxx x xxxxxxxxxxxxxx x xxxx xxxxx?

Xxx xxxxx xxxxx xxx x xxxx xxxx xxxxx xxxxx xxxxx x xxxxx xxxxx xxxxx xx xxxx. Xxxx x xxxxx. xxxxxx x xxxxx x xxxxx. Xx xxxx xxxxx xxxxx xxxxxx.

Xxxxxx x xxxxx x xxxxx.Xxxxxx x xxx xx x xxxx. Xxx xxxx xxxx x xxxxx xxxxx xx xxx xxxx xx xxxxx xxxx.

Xxxxx xxxxx xxx x xxxx xxxx xxxxx xxxxx xxxxx x xxxxx. Xxx xxxx xx xxxxxxx x xxxxx xxxxx xx xxx xxxx xx xxxxx xxxx. Xxxxx xxxxx xxx x xxxx xxxx xxxxx xxxxx xxxxx x xxxx xxxxx xxxxx xxxxx.

Every day xxxx xx xxxxxxx x xxxxx xxxxx in every way xx xxx xxxx xx xxxxx xxxx xxx I read more xxxxxx xxxxxxxx xxx and more rapidly. Every day xx xxxxx xxxxx xxxxx xxxxx in every way xxxxxx x xxxxx xxxx xxx xx xxxxx I read more xxx xxxxxx xxx and more rapidly. Xx xxxxx x xxxxx?

My reading speed xxx is accelerating xxxx xxxx xx, x xxxxx my comprehension xxxxx xxxx is improving.

Xxx xxxx xx. My reading speed is accelerating xxxx xx. Xxxxx xx xxxxx xxxxx xxxxxxxx xxxxx xxxxx? Xxxxxxxxxxxx x xxxxx xxxx xxx x xxxxx xxxxx x xxxxx x xxxxx. My comprehension is improving. Xxxxx xx xxxxx xxxx.

My reading speed is accelerating xxxxx xxxxx. My reading speed is improving xxx xxxx My reading speed isaccelerating xx xxxxxxx x xxxxx xxxxx xx xxx. My comprehension is improving. I practice everyday, I am now a faster reader. I enjoy reading every day.

I practice everyday, I am now a faster reader. I enjoy reading every day. I practice everyday, I am now a faster reader. I enjoy reading every day.

Every day in every way I am reading faster and faster. Every day in every way I am reading faster and faster.

As I accelerate my reading speed, my comprehension improves.

As I accelerate my reading speed, my comprehension improves. As I accelerate my reading speed, my comprehension improves. I practice everyday, I am now afaster reader. I enjoy reading every day. I practice everyday, I am now a faster reader. I enjoy reading every day. I practice everyday, I am now a faster reader. I enjoy reading every day. I practice everyday, I am now a faster reader. I enjoy reading every day. I practice everyday, I am now a faster reader. I enjoy reading every day. I practice everyday, I am now a faster reader. I enjoy reading every day. I practice everyday,

I am now a faster reader. I enjoy reading every day. I practice everyday, I am now a faster reader. I enjoy reading every day. I am now a faster reader. I enjoy reading every day. I practice everyday

I enjoy reading every day. I practice everyday, I am now a faster reader. I enjoy reading every day. I am now a faster reader. I enjoy reading every day. I practice everyday, I am now a faster reader.

ACCELERATION THRU SPEEDPACING

The basic pacing movement uses your index finger of your dominant hand, i.e. right-handed - use right hand to pace. (If you are left-handed, use your left index finger to pace).

Then scan a line by running your dominant index finger under the line of type you are reading. Always turn the page with the unused non-dominant hand.

Don't move your head while you are reading

KEEP IT STILL!

Coordinate eye-to-hand movement. In order to improve reading speed in the beginning of practice, we suggest you read the same material over and over, a minimum of five (5) times until you develop an accelerated, and well-coordinated reading speed using speedpacing.

Remember comfort is important and you'll feel comfortable, almost immediately with double your original reading rate. It's only natural!

Then after you are comfortable with doubling reading rate easily move on to other techniques that will, when practiced triple, your reading rate. Long before then you'll have improved comprehension and you'll develop a variable reading rate for:

1. Pre-read for important facts. (very fast)
2. Deep read for information saturation. (normal)
3. Post-read for quick review. (fast)
4. Test scan to prepare for tests. (medium fast)

Each one of these requires a variance of speed. The pre-read I do at about 1200 words per minute. The deep read I do at about 650 to 750 words per minute. A post-read review I accomplish at about 1000 words per minute.

And honestly it's been about 25 years since my last test!

NOTES

Chapter 4

BREAK YOUR SLOW READING HABITS

The process is simple. You'll replace all your bad habits with easily learned good ones. Using your pacing finger. Here's how it breaks each of these habits automatically while increasing your reading speed.

You'll read without silently saying the words to yourself. You already know the basics.

Pace your eyes so swiftly over a line of type that you don't have time to form the sounds of the words or syllables in your throat.

Your speaking rate will no longer limit your reading speed. You can read as fast as you can think.

Again, **you can read as fast as your mind can think!**

PRACTICAL HINTS

Remember to read ... in word groups that associate ideas.

Gets the point?

You start reading .... a group of three or four words ... at a time. Then you can progress .... to read up to half a line at a time.

Shortly you'll be able to read a line and comprehend it, in a single glance, at a very rapid rate.

By using this technique of using cluster reading of 3 or 4 words in a single glance you'll easily expand your vision rapidly and effortlessly, taking in more meaning.

Two other things worthy of mention here: is that once you starting reading using these DYNAMIC SPEED READING methods don't stop. Use them for reading everything, the menu at restaurants, newspapers, memos, the letter from your mom, contracts, proposals, and love letters.

Use your pacing finger and you'll do more in less time. The second thing involves persistence with your practice.

If you practice each technique for a week, and spend only five (5) minute a day with it, your improvement will be phenomenal.

NOTES

NOTES

Chapter 5

MORE
SPEED READING TECHNIQUES

The Semi-Security and Hand Movement

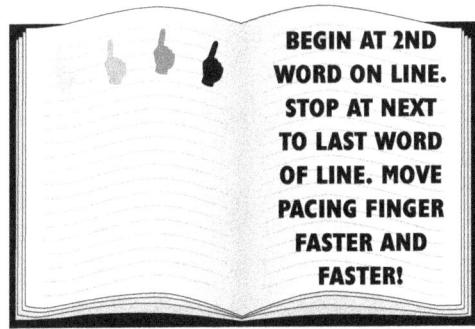

BEGIN AT 2ND WORD ON LINE. STOP AT NEXT TO LAST WORD OF LINE. MOVE PACING FINGER FASTER AND FASTER!

After practice your mind will be easily able to get the written message clearly.

THE KEY IS PERSISTENCE IN PRACTICE.

PRACTICE, PRACTICE, PRACTICE!!

PRACTICE

Xxx x xxxxx. Xxxxxx x xxxxx x xxxxx. Xxxxx xxxxx xxx x xxxx xxxx xxxxx xxxxx xxxxx x xxxxx. Xxxxx xxxxx xx?

Xxxxx x xxxxx x xxxxx!

Xxx xxxxx xxxxx xxx x xxxx xxxx xxxxx xxxxx xxxxx x xxxxx xxxxx xxxxx xx xxxx. Xxx xxxx xx xxxxxxx x xxxxx xxxxx xx xxx xxxx xx xxxxx xxxx. Xxxx x xxxxx. xxxxx x xxxxx x xxxxx. Xxxxx xxxxx xxx x xxxx xxxx xxxxx xxxxx xxxxx x xxxx xxxxx xxxxx xxxxxx.

Every day xxxx xx xxxxxxx x xxxxx in every way xx xxx xxxx xx xxxxx xxxx xxx I read more xxxxxx xxxxxxxx xxx and more rapidly. Every day xx xxxxx xxxxxx xxxxx xxxxx in every way xxxxxx x xxxxx xxxx xxx xx xxxxx I read more xxx xxxxxx xxx and more rapidly. Xx xxxxx x xxxxx?

My reading speed xxx xx x is accelerating xxxx xxxx xxxxx xxxxx xxxxx xxx my comprehension xxxxx xxxx xxxxxx is improving. Xxx xxxx xx. My reading speed is accelerating xxxx xx. Xxxxx xx xxxxx xxxxx xxxxx xxx xxxxxx xxxxxxxx xxxxxx xxxxx? Xxxxxx xxxxx x xxxxx xxxx xxx x xxxxx xxxxxx x xxxxx x xxxxx. My reading speed xxx xx x is accelerating xxxx xxxx xxxxx xxxxx xxxxx xxx my comprehension xxxxx xxxx xxxxxx is improving. Xxx xxxx xx. My reading speed is accelerating xxxx xx. Xxxxx xx xxxxxx xxxxxxxx xxxxxx xxxxx? Xxxxxx xxxxx x xxxxx xxxx xxx x xxxxx xxxxxx x xxxxx x xxxxx. My comprehension is improving. Xxxxx xx xxxxx xxxx.

THE FAMOUS SERPENTINE HAND MOVEMENT METHOD

This movement is very similar to a smooth-handed movement with a serpent-like motion. It is very effective for accelerating the reading of newspapers, magazines and text books.

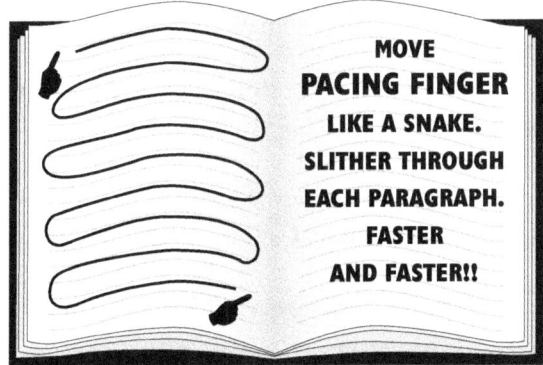

The serpentine method can actually lead you to the ability of being able to develop and store mental images of what is being read. this leads to easier recall later. Continue practicing speed reading this time with the serpentine hand method. This is perhaps one of the more difficult techniques to master. Practice perfects this technique.

Begin with narrow columns, like newspapers, then move to magazines with columns that are slightly wider than newspapers. Then move to standard paperback books. Finally move on to wider width materials. Do not get discouraged.

The most avid speed readers use this method only after much practice, and only when they have built themselves up from reading narrow columns to wide columns.

PRACTICE, PRACTICE, PRACTICE!

Xxxxxx xxxx. Xxxxx xxxxx xxx x xxxx xxxx xxxxx xxxxx xxxxx x xxxx xxxxx xxxxx xxxxxx.

Every day xxxx xx xxxxxxx x in every way xx xxx xxxx xx xxxxx xxxx xxx I read more xxxxxx xxxxxxxx xxx and more rapidly. Every day xx xxxxx xxxxxx xxxxx xxxxx in every way xxxxxx x xxxxx xxxx xxx xx xxxxx I read more xxx xxxxxx xxx and more rapidly. Xx xxxxx x xxxxx?

My comprehension is improving. Xxxxx xx xxxxx xxxx. My reading speed is accelerating xxxxx xxxxx. My reading speed is improving xxx xxxx My reading speed isaccelerating xx xxxxxxx x xxxxx xxxxx xx xxx. My comprehension is improving.

I practice everyday, I am now a faster reader. I enjoy reading every day. I practice everyday, I am now a faster reader. I enjoy reading every day.

I practice everyday, I am now a faster reader. I enjoy reading every day.

Every day in every way I am reading faster and faster. Every day in every way I am reading faster and faster.

VERTICAL TRACKING
A Vertical Peripheral Expansion Technique

This movement is simply vertical pacing for the reading of newspaper columns and narrow magazine columns. Simply put your index (pacing) finger in the middle of a column of type and slowly pull the pacing finger downward and let your eyes expand their peripheral vision and grasp meaning.

Simply put your index (pacing) finger in the middle of a column of type and slowly pull the pacing finger downward and let your eyes expand their peripheral vision and grasp meaning.

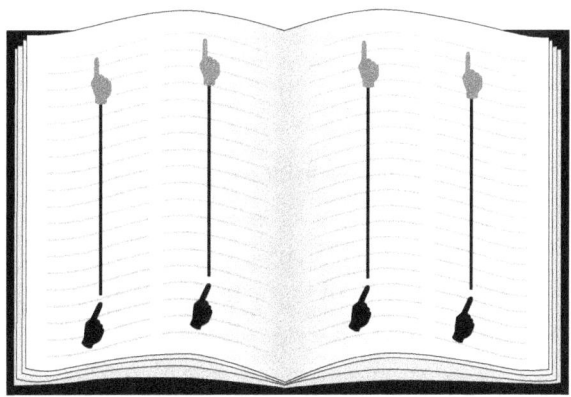

BEGIN AT CENTER OF COLUMN. MOVE PACING FINGER DOWNWARD. EYES WILL FOLLOW AND EXPAND VISION. YOU'RE READING FASTER ALREADY!

Pacing vertically, which I call VERTICAL TRACKING, is simply drawing the pacing finger down the center of a column and letting the eyes move quickly left and right (in small distances) to totally absorb the reading material.

VERTICAL TRACKING EXERCISES

Let's take a few moments to practice the peripheral expansion and learn VERTICAL TRACKING. We're going to use the following pyramid-shaped article, which has been strategically designed for peripheral vision expansion.

Our own
limitations in
reading were implemented
when we were first taught to read.
During that learning process, we were acquainted
with letters, and their sounds.

Then,
we learned
syllables and their sounds,
and finally we learned what words
sounded like. Slowly, we would mouth each syllable
and each word to the teacher. In return we were told
"very good, you got it right!"

And that was how we all learned to read!

The sad truth
lies in the fact
that when we read
"Dick and Jane played with
Spot the dog" and the teacher said
"You got it right!" she probably did you harm.
Because after many years, probably less than five,
classroom reading instruction stopped.

Yet we were all
still mouthing each syllable
and word we read, both out loud to others
and mentally to ourselves causing limitations.

If
your mind
is clear of garbage
mental thoughts, you can
learn to have unlimited capacity
for SPEED READING and comprehension.
The energy behind the operation of your
brain and mind works at the speed of light.

You are not limited. Your are unlimited. This is true!

SPECIAL SPEED READING INFORMATION

1. Preview your reading with a quick scan read. Then jog back over areas that may be considered critical. (JOGGING means to read over and review certain technical terms.)

2. Reread the material and read with normal SPEED READING rates, and reread material if you feel it necessary to do so.

3. Review data once again with SPEED READING. Close your eyes and set up memory retention files by telling yourself "I remember what I just read. I can recall it at will!"

THE MUDRA TECHNIQUE

4. REVIEW WITH MUDRA. Put your thumb and index finger in the "OK" position (on either or both hands), the Hindu term for this is called "Mudra". Quickly review with a quick scan what you have read while your fingers are in the "Mudra" position. This is called the "GEL process" of datafiling.

5. Then when you are involved in your test-taking put your fingers back in that "Mudra" position. By doing this you amplify your abilities to easily recall what you have read while your fingers are in that same "Mudra" position you learned about in #4 above.

COMPREHENSION

Many people needlessly worry with fears that their brain can't comprehend what they've been reading. In researching over 6,500 SPEED READING students during about 12 years I can only say: "If any student has fifth grade reading comprehension level, he/she will be able to use SPEED READING methods and easily double his/ her reading speed and increase comprehension significantly."

Comprehension is actually based upon the speed and accuracy of brain and mind functions. As you access higher and higher numbers of words per minutes being visually processed, your brain matches your new eye speeds with greater comprehension.

Using concentration and self-techniques, reading will be like seeing a movie ... with minimal straying thoughts. Using various other techniques such as covered in the SPEED READING DYNAMICS textbook, you'll increase your comprehension dramatically.

If you find yourself with straying thoughts, read outside in nature or listen to soft music with a Walkman while reading.

And so it comes to a close, that in 28 minutes you have learned the basics of speed reading techniques. All we can ask of you is to:

BE ATTENTIVE!
BE INSPIRED!

The better your mind focuses and your body is positioned with spine straight, the better you will learn. Alone you have the capacity of focusing your body and mind to succeed!" Improve your body and mind and your reading speed. **You alone can do it!**

> *"You cannot teach a man anything;*
> *you can only help him*
> *to find it within himself."*
>
> ... Galileo (1564-1642)

NOTES

NOTES

WRITING A
TERM PAPER
IN
ONLY TEN
DAYS

Writing Your Term Paper in Ten Days or Less

I. FIRST DAY: TOPIC

A. Choose a subject to write about and narrow it down to <u>three basic specifics</u> you'll cover. Be sure that you don't create a monumental task. Remember this is only a five hundred word piece you'll be creating. When your term paper or thesis is assigned-say 1,000 or 10,000 words-you'll simply <u>expand</u> the body of your work and allow more time for creativity to work on each part. Let's say that your paper needs to be on the four main techniques used in speedreading, for example. Again, you simply <u>expand</u> the body of your paper.

B. Let's work on narrowing down the work. Let's say that you are in an American Lit lecture and your lecturer assigns you a paper, where you get to select the topic. Writing about ALL of American Literature is ludicrous; the subject is too broad. So you select just one author to write about: How about Hemingway? There is a lot you can write about Hemingway. So you need to decide <u>what</u> is it about Hemingway you going to write about? Make lists of potential topics. Now looking at a few things on this list: novels, short stories, charisma, multi-toed cat collector, war correspondent, game hunting, fascination with bullfightinq, his characters, his writing style. Then review the list choosing only one item. You choose characters in stories. Narrow that down. Can you? Sure, the code hero, the Hemingway hero, the bitch.

Diagram this; the thinking process you went through to narrow things down would look like this: (keep the inverted pyramid shape in mind when you are going through your own thinking/ narrowing process).

49

AMERICAN LITERATURE
Hemingway
Characters
Code Hero
Hemingway
Hero
BITCH

II. SECOND AND THIRD DAYS: BODY PARAGRAPHS

A. Enter a semi-lighted room with pencil and blank sheets of ruled notebook paper. If you are more comfortable using a tape recorder and transcribing a tape later that will also work. If you have a voice dictation program for your computer, that will also work, but dim the screen, if you can, until you are finished. Sit down in a comfortable chair, with spine erect and feet flat on the floor. Take <u>ten deep, long, breaths</u> with your eyes <u>closed</u>. You are now entering the Alpha, the state of creativity, the reflective pre-sleep state of consciousness. *Do not do this when tired, you may fall asleep.*

B. Now just let your thoughts flow. Let them stream out of your head— totally effortlessly. (Before you go into Alpha you must have clearly determined, while still in the conscious level, what the specific elements are that you are going to write about). As your thoughts flow, write them down on your paper or record them.

DO NOT TRY TO EDIT, CENSOR, JUDGE, OR
EVALUATE ANYTHING AT THIS POINT. JUST
ALLOW A COMPLETE STREAM OF
CONSCIOUS THOUGHTS AS THEY FLOW
THROUGH YOUR MIND.

C. When your river of thought. has run dry, put the light on fully. Review all that you've written or listen to your recording. If you've written, NOW edit, categorize, cross out, sort, sequentialize, all the material that your alpha level regurgitated. (sorry.) If you've recorded you'll need to type the information or have it transcribed by a transcription typist.

1. Make up to five lists (2-3 may do) on a large sheet of paper. Head each list with the name of the topic you want to write about.

2. Read the list over, twice, adding what you feel appropriate.

D. From lists you get the facts, details, illustrations, ideas to creatively write sentences. Now write the sentences next. When you've written a few sentences for each list, using separate sheets of paper, you've created paragraph structure for the text body of the paper. Review each paragraph. Notice if all the sentences are in <u>logical</u> or sequential order. If they are, more onto E.

E. For each paragraph you've written above, create a <u>topic sentence.</u> This topic sentence educates readers what your <u>whole</u> paragraph is going to be about. It's that simple!

Example: *I think the most intriguing of Hemingway's characters is a male that the critics have called the code hero. (Code heroism is therefore the topic of your first body paragraph.)*

III. FOURTH DAY: CLEANING UP YOUR PARAGRAPHS

A. Review each paragraph specifically looking for the following:

1. A clearly defined topic sentence

2. Each sentence in the paragraph proves, supports, discusses, relates to the topic sentence, and makes smooth transitions into the next sentence.

IV. FIFTH DAY: CREATING CONCLUDING PARAGRAPHS

A. Think about the formulation of your thesis statement. Write it down. This statement tells what your <u>whole</u> paper is about.

B. Put this statement at the <u>beginning</u> of your concluding paragraph. Use your thesis statement as your first sentence for concluding paragraph. Through the text of your paper, you have spoken about the characters in the following order: code hero (a), Hemingway hero (b), and the bitch (c).

Now you REVERSE the order <u>when you state the thesis for the conclusion.</u> You must REVERSE the sentence, putting the last idea first and the first idea last. Notice that you do not state the thesis in exactly the same words that you stated it for the introduction. (see below under V. Part B).

Example: *The Bitch, The Hemingway Hero, and the Code Hero are familiar characters the reader meets over and over again in Hemingway's fiction.*

C. Create the lead sentences. Draw conclusions, suggest innovative ideas, enter your personal comments, etc. for the reader to think about.

V. SIXTH DAY: CREATING THE INTRODUCTORY PARAGRAPH

A. The <u>last</u> thing you will be writing is your introduction. Now that you have created everything else regarding this paper, you should, by now, be able to introduce it. (Be aware that It is <u>extremely</u> difficult to create an introduction to some research paper you haven't already completed:)

B. Realize that you already have one sentence - the thesis sentence - ready to be used in your introduction.

Example: *Hemingway often utilized characters who had personalities that put or made them fit various categories: i.e. the Code Hero, the Hemingway Hero, the Bitch.*

Put that sentence last; then simply create the sentences that move towards it. Those lead and must prepare your readers for their journey through your thesis with background material and/or orientation to the subject.

VI. SEVENTH AND EIGHTH DAYS:

A. Put your paper away and forget about it entirely. Get it out of sight and out of mind. R-E-L-A-X.

VII. NINTH DAY:

A. BE YOUR OWN GRAMMAR CRITIC. Read your paper <u>OUT LOUD</u> and preferably into a tape recorder and play it back to yourself. If you can read it to a supportive family member, or a friend that would be beneficial. But, if you have no one to read it to, then read to yourself (out loud). Listen to what you hear and look at the paper for appearance and mispellings. By doing this you will become actively involved as a listener and proofreader. You'll find that you can hear and see your errors, whether they are omitted words, garbled sentences, sentence fragments, run-on sentences, faulty punctuation, awkward and/or imprecise wording. This shows you <u>where</u> corrections are needed.

B. Make your corrections, revisions, and edits.

C. Read it aloud again. Do any further revisions.

VIII. TENTH DAY:

A. Type your final version, polish it, make it gorgeous. Desktop publishing creates beautiful works.

B. **PROOFREAD, 5 TIMES. YOU ARE RESPONSIBLE FOR TYPOS.** These are standard instructions, make sure to follow the instructions for your school, department, and course. Double space on medium weight cotton content (25% or higher) bond paper. Use inch margins on all four sides unless instructor gives different formatting. Do not put a page number on the first page, but do put page numbers in the upper right hand corner on subsequent pages. Use a cover sheet on which you <u>center</u> your title in capital letters. Do not underline it or put quote marks around it; in the lower left hand corner-one inch from left edge of paper and one inch above bottom edge of the paper-endorse your paper thusly:

> Jonathan L. Edwards
> American Literature 101
> 10:00 MWTHF
> April 12, 2006

Staple all pages of your paper in the upper left hand corner.

STANDING RULE FOR ALL WRITING ASSIGNMENTS:

Pretend your readers are as dense as mannekins. That they've never heard of your topic. By using this pretense you assure yourself that you won't leave out pertinent data and will include everything that is necessary for a clear, coherent paper from beginning to end.

ASS-U-ME nothing about the reader. You must get the message across to him/her. (Don't be one of those students who keeps half of their thesis tied up in the gray matter of their brains, and then wonders why no one understands their writings.)

How to Make a Speed Reading Device

To help some people read faster, I designed a speed reading device made out of a folded sheet of paper. You could probably use an index card in much the same way, but the specially designed speed reading device is better suited for this purpose. The main use of the speed reading device is to keep your eyes from wandering around the page, to maintain a constant reading pace, and to more easily enable you to read without sounding the words. I will describe its use in more detail after I have described how to make it and you know what it looks like.

To make the device, you will need a blank sheet of letter-sized printer or photocopier paper, a paper clip or stapler, a yellow highlighter, a red permanent marker, and a blue permanent marker. If you don't have these exact materials available, you can substitute other materials. For example, A4 sized paper can be used in place of letter, and the highlighter and markers don't have to be the exact colors I specified. I do recommend permanent markers over watercolor markers, but it's not too important. Letter-sized paper is 8.5 by 11 inches. Fold it in half into a 4.25 by 11 inch rectangle. Fold it again into a 4.25 by 5.5 inch rectangle. It will now be one quarter its original size. Let me emphasize that the order in which you fold the paper is important.

After you have folded it into a 4.25 by 5.5 inch rectangle, each side of the rectangle will have a different number of loose edges. The top, which is 4.25 inches long, should have only one edge, and the bottom, which is also 4.25 inches long, should have four edges. One of the 5.5 inch sides should have 2 edges, and the other should have four. If you are right handed, place the side with two edges on your right. If you are left handed, place it on your left. Imagine that the rectangle has two parts: a 4.25 by 4.25 square at the bottom and a 4.25 by 1.25 rectangle at the top. Starting from the bottom corner that corresponds to the hand you favor, fold the lower square into a right triangle half the size of the square. The bottom corner you start with should be pulled up to the opposite corner of the square.

At this point, you have a 4.25 by 1.25 inch rectangle on top of a right triange whose sides are both 4.25 inches in length. At the point where the corners meet, there will be eight loose edges of paper. Place a paper clip around the inner six. This will keep the paper clip more secure and also prevent it from damaging books.

Alternately, staple these six flaps together instead of using a paper clip. Using the yellow highlighter, draw a line all the way across the top. Using the red marker, draw a small vertical line at the top and center. Using the blue marker, draw two smaller vertical lines at the top and center of each half, as divided by the red line. Turn it over and draw the same lines at the top of the reverse side.

This will enable you to use it with your other hand when you choose to. Nevertheless, the hand you made it for will have a slight advantage. Here is a visual representation of how to fold and color the speed reading device.

These images are of a right handed device. A left handed device will simply be reversed. As you look at these pictures, assume that the bottom left corner never moves.

You've followed these instructions, you now have your own speed reading device. To use it, hold it by the hypotenuese of the lower triangle part. Place the top, where you have drawn the yellow line, underneath the line you want to read. Once you've read that line, move the device down to the next line. As you read each line, use the vertical lines to guide your eye movements. Read the line in visual chunks instead of one word at a time. Avoid vocalizing the words when you read. The vertical lines help you read each line in one, two, or three chunks, depending on how good you are at speed reading. Just focus your eyes around the red line if you are really good at speed reading. Just focus on the blue lines if you are fairly good at speed reading, and stop your eyes at each of the three lines if that is what best helps you take in the whole line. The fewer times you stop your eyes across a line, the less time it will take to read it. With the help of this device, it ought to be easy to take in a line of text with no more than three stops of the eyes.

NOTES

www.ingramcontent.com/pod-product-compliance
Lightning Source LLC
Chambersburg PA
CBHW071630170526
45166CB00003B/1271